BOLD KIDS

Ancient Greece

ANCIENT HISTORY FACTS AND PICTURE BOOK FOR CHILDREN

No part of this book may be reproduced or used in any way or form or by any means whether electronic or mechanical, this means that you cannot record or photocopy any material ideas or tips that are provided in this book.

Copyright 2022

All images in this book have been reproduced with the knowledge and prior consent of the artists concerned, and no responsibility is accepted by producer, publisher, or printer for any infringement of copyright or otherwise, arising from the contents of this publication.

In fact, many people think that Ancient Greece was a country, but it was not. Instead, it was a collection of city-states, each with a ruler. The most important cities were at the centre, such as Athens, which was famous for its theaters.

The cities were also populated by gods and mythical monsters. For example, the three-headed dog Cerberus, the Medusa, and the Cyclops, which had one eye on the forehead.

The ancient Greeks had a rich culture. They celebrated their gods through festivals. The first Olympics were held in 776 B.C., and they're believed to have been the inspiration for the modern Olympics.

The winners were rewarded with wreaths of leaves and free meals for life, and they had the best seats in the theater. The Greeks also placed statues of their gods and goddesses in temples. Some of their most famous temples are the Parthenon and the Acropolis.

The ancient Greeks also made some of the world's most famous marbles. Marble from Greece is still used today, including the statues of the gods. It's also interesting to know that the Greek language is incredibly rich.

As a result, there are thousands of words in the English language. It was also an agricultural country, and the Minoans had a bull-leaping competition. The sport involved gymnastic vaults over a fierce bull.

Athens had no president or prime minister. Their chief officials were called archons and were elected by lot. The Athens Assembly was the highest authority for deciding the laws of the citystate.

This assembly met on the Pnyx hill, west of the Acropolis, and was attended by all adult male citizens. Only five out of over thirty thousand men were allowed to vote, and voting was by show of hands.

In addition to the Greek civilization, the ancient Greeks had a lot of pets. Dogs were the most common pets of the ancient Greeks. They also had horses and thrones. These animals were very useful for hunting, and the Olympic games were a big part of their lives.

They ruled the world. However, the civilization was not without its problems. The Greeks' religion was based on the belief in many gods. There were 12 gods in Ancient Greece, and they were usually consulted on disputes.

The Greeks invented the theatre. In some cities, there were theaters with capacity for as many as fifteen thousand people. Only males and boys were allowed to perform on stage.

Actors wore masks to show their emotions, which were sometimes two-sided. The ancient Greeks wore chitons, which were robes made of one piece of cotton. The slaves wore loincloths.

A great example of democracy is the idea that a government is run by the people. This was considered a revolutionary idea in ancient Greece, but only a few percent of the population were allowed to participate.

The people were not unified, but rather a group of city-states. Athens was the most powerful, and many of the other cities were more akin to a kingdom. They also had a variety of different religions, which included Christians and Jews.

The ancient Greeks believed in many different gods. They believed in magical creatures and believed that they were able to interact with humans. They built temples and honored their gods. They also prayed all the time, in the form of a religious service.

They loved to compete with each other and adored the Olympics. They would hold meetings on Mount Olympus and resolve disputes. During the summer, these gods would rule over their region.

While the ancient Greeks were not a nation, they were a civilization. They were very sophisticated and influenced many aspects of human life, including art and philosophy. They were famous for their inventions and innovations.

Their history is a fascinating story that is full of wonders. Not only were they rich, but they were also very kind. And they lived in a city where dogs were the most common pets.

Ingram Content Group UK Ltd.
Milton Keynes UK
UKHW052338030423
419480UK00008B/89